Soulful Slow Cooker: 60 Super #Delish Soul Food Inspired Crock Pot Recipes

RHONDA BELLE

Copyright © 2016 Rhonda Belle

All rights reserved.

ISBN-13: 978-1540401823

ISBN-10: 1540401820

DEDICATION

To Foodies Everywhere…Enjoy & Be Well!

Table of Contents

Soulful Slow Cooking 8
   Apple & Brown Sugar Corned Beef 8
   Apple Glazed Pork Roast 8
   Apple-Coconut Crisp 9
   Autumn Chicken 9
   Bayou Gumbo 10
   Beautiful Baked Apples 10
   Bee My Honey Chicken Wings 11
   Beefy Brunch Casserole 11
   Best Barbecued Meatballs 11
   Broccoli & Cheese Soup 12
   Cabbage Bake 12
   Candied Bananas 13
   Carrot Pudding 13
   Cherry Cobbler 13
   Chicken Casserole 14
   Chicken Sensation 14
   Chocolate Brownie Pudding Cake 14
   Chops in a Crock 15
   Cola Basted Ham 15
   Cold Season Chicken Soup 15
   Country Citrus Fish 16
   Cranberry Holiday Pork Roast 16
   Crazy Cajun Pecans 16
   Cream of Sweet Potato Soup 17
   Creamed Chicken & Rice 17
   Creamy Red Potatoes 18
   Crockpot Black-Eyed Peas 18
   Crockpot Chicken & Dumplings 18
   Crockpot Clam Bisque 19
   Crockpot Jambalaya 19
   Curried Fruit Bake 20
   Down Home Sausage & Rice 20
   Family Reunion Potato Salad 20

Garlic Chicken & Cabbage 21
Ham & Cheese Casserole 21
Hamburger Casserole 21
Home-Style Bread Pudding 22
Hoppin' Shrimp Creole..22
Hot 'N' Spicy Peanuts..22
Jammin' Jerk Chicken 23
Lemon Baked Chicken 23
Lemon-Garlic Chicken 23
Maple Sweet Potatoes 24
Melty Mac & Cheese 24
Old-Fashioned Chicken Noodle Soup (Low-fat) 24
Orange Glazed Chicken (Low-Fat) 25
Peach Crisp 25
Salmon Bake 25
Saturday Night Dump Dinner 26
Savory Corn Cake...26
Seafood Chowder 27
Simple Sunday Roast..27
Slow-Cooker Candy 27
Southern Barbecue Chicken 28
Southern Style Green Bean & Potato Casserole...28
Spicy BBQ Beef Stew 28
Split Pea Soup 29
Spoon Peaches 29
Tasty Tenderloin Tips 29
Vegetable Beef Soup 30

ACKNOWLEDGEMENTS

To the love of my life, Johnny.
You are Mommy's greatest inspiration.

To my Mom & Dad (Sunset February 2016)
Love you both...always!

Soulful Slow Cooking

Soul food cooking is a just plain good cooking! The taste, the warmth, the comfort are all the result of a healthy dose of seasoning, natural flavors and love. Yet, there are those occasions when time is limited and the traditional taste of home cooking is still desired. The slow cooker (or Crock Pot) offers a convenient way for you to enjoy the taste you love with a set it and forget it method of cooking.

Prep your ingredients at night and start a slow cooker cycle before dashing out the door for work. You'll walk into the house welcomed by the perfume of Southern winters and grandma's house. Indulge in these wonderful soulful recipes for everything from soups to casseroles to entrees to sweets. This collection is perfect for busy cooks like you!

Apple & Brown Sugar Corned Beef
½ head cabbage, cut into chunks
1 corned beef brisket
1 cup brown sugar
1 onion, peeled and chopped
1 quart apple juice
1 tablespoon prepared mustard
2 medium carrots, pared and cut into chunks
8 small red potatoes

Place all ingredients in large crock pot (cut meat in half if necessary). Stir to mix. Cook on high for 4 to 5 hours on high (or 8 to 10 hours on low). Remove meat and vegetables and some of the cooking liquid. Slice meat thinly across the grain. Serve with cornbread, the veggies and savory beef gravy made by the meat. #Delish!

Apple Glazed Pork Roast
¼ cup apple juice
1 teaspoon ground ginger
3 tablespoons brown sugar
4 lbs. pork loin roast
6 ripe apples (variety of your choice)

Rub roast with salt and pepper. Brown pork roast under broiler to remove excess fat; drain well. Core and quarter apples. Place apple quarters in bottom of the slow cooker. Place roast on top of apples. Combine apple juice, brown sugar, and ginger. Spoon over top of roast to moisten. Cover and cook on low for 10-12 hours until done. #Delish!

Apple-Coconut Crisp

½ cup butterscotch or caramel ice cream topping
½ cup quick rolled oats
½ cup sweetened flaked coconut
½ teaspoon cinnamon
1 tablespoon flour
1/3 cup brown sugar
1/3 cup flour
2 tablespoons butter or margarine
4 large Granny Smith apples, peeled and sliced

Combine apples with coconut, 1 tablespoon flour, 1/3 cup brown sugar, and cinnamon in slow cooker. Drizzle with the ice cream topping. Combine remaining ingredients in a small bowl with a fork and sprinkle over apple mixture. Cover and cook on high for 2½ to 3 hours until apples are tender. Serve warm with vanilla ice cream or doused with Cool Whip. #Delish!

Autumn Chicken

1 (14.5 ounces) can of chicken broth
1 acorn squash, skin removed
2 carrots
2 large (or 4 small) chicken breasts
2 parsnips
3 tablespoons garlic, chopped
Honey
Nutmeg
Pepper
Salt

Peel and chop carrots and parsnips and place them in the bottom of the slow cooker. Sprinkle with garlic and place chicken on top of veggies. Pour in broth. Cut squash into chunks and place on top of chicken. Sprinkle desired amounts of salt, pepper and nutmeg on top of squash and drizzle enough honey on top to lightly cover the squash. Cook on low 8-10 hours. Serve hot and enjoy!

Bayou Gumbo

¼ teaspoon ground cayenne red pepper
¼ teaspoon ground black pepper
½ pound smoked sausage, cut into ½ inch slices
1 (12 ounce) package shelled, deveined, rinsed and cooked medium shrimp
1 (14.5 ounce) can diced tomatoes, undrained
1½ cups uncooked regular long-grain white rice
1 large green bell pepper, chopped
1 large onion, chopped
2 cups frozen cut okra
3 cups water
3 garlic cloves, minced
3 tablespoons oil
3 tablespoons all-purpose flour

In small saucepan, combine flour and oil; mix well. Cook, stirring constantly, over medium-high heat for 5 minutes. Reduce heat to medium; cook, stirring constantly, about 10 minutes or until mixture turns reddish brown. Place flour-oil mixture in 3 ½ to 4 quart slow cooker. Stir in all remaining ingredients except shrimp, rice and water. Cover and cook on low setting for 7-9 hours. When ready to serve, cook rice in a saucepan. Meanwhile, add shrimp to gumbo mixture in slow cooker; mix well. Cover and cook on low setting for additional 20 minutes. Serve gumbo over rice. #Delish!

Beautiful Baked Apples

¼ teaspoon cinnamon
½ cup brown sugar
¾ cup orange juice
¾ cup rose wine
1 teaspoon lemon rind grated
2 teaspoons grated orange rind
6 large cooking apples
Whipped cream

Remove core from apples and place in slow cooker. Mix together all other ingredients, except whipped cream. Pour over apples, cover cooker and set to low for about 3 ½ hours or until apples are tender. Cool and serve with whipped cream. #Delish!

Bee My Honey Chicken Wings
½ cups soy sauce
½ garlic clove, minced
1 cup honey
2 tablespoons ketchup
2 tablespoons vegetable oil
3 lbs. chicken wings (drummies or cut whole wings)
Salt & pepper to taste

Cut off and discard chicken wing tips. Cut each wing into 2 parts (if working with whole wings) and sprinkle with salt and pepper. Combine remaining ingredients and mix well. Place wings in slow cooker and pour mixed sauce over meat. Cook 6 to 8 hours on low. Simple & #Delish!

Beefy Brunch Casserole
¼ cup scalded milk
½ cup sharp cheddar cheese, grated
½ package frozen chopped spinach, thawed and drained
½ teaspoon nutmeg
½ teaspoon oregano
1½ lbs. ground beef
1 large onion, finely chopped
2 garlic cloves, minced
2 tablespoons olive oil or butter
2 teaspoons salt
3 tablespoons flour
4 ounces mushrooms, sliced
6 large eggs, well beaten

In skillet, lightly brown ground beef and onion in olive oil; drain well. Sauté mushrooms in just a bit of the oil left in the pan. Place all in well-greased crock pot. Stir in remaining ingredients (except eggs, milk and cheese) until well blended. Beat eggs and milk together. Pour over other ingredients; stir well. Dust with additional nutmeg. Cover and cook on low setting for 7 to 10 hours or until firm. Just before serving, sprinkle with grated cheese. #Delish!

Best Barbecued Meatballs
¼ cup cider vinegar
¼ cup reduced-sodium soy sauce
½ teaspoon black pepper
¾ teaspoon garlic salt
1 1/3 cups ketchup, divided
1½ teaspoon hot pepper sauce
1 cup packed brown sugar

1 can (6 ounces) tomato paste
1 egg, slightly beaten
2 lbs. lean ground beef
2 tablespoons dried onion flakes
3 tablespoons seasoned dry bread crumbs

Preheat oven to 350 degrees. Combine ground beef, 1/3 cup ketchup, bread crumbs, egg onion flakes, garlic sale, and black pepper in medium bowl. Mix lightly but thoroughly; shape into 1-inch meatballs. Place meatballs in two shallow roasting pans and bake 18 minutes or until browned. Transfer meatballs to slow cooker. Mix remaining 1 cup ketchup, sugar, tomato paste, soy sauce, vinegar, and hot pepper sauce in medium bowl. Pour over meatballs. Cover and cook on low 4 hours. Enjoy!

Broccoli & Cheese Soup

1 (10 ounce) package frozen chopped broccoli, thawed
1 tablespoon flour
2 cups cooked egg noodles
2 cups shredded American cheese
2 tablespoons butter
3 tablespoons chopped onions
5 ½ cups milk
Salt to taste

Combine all ingredients in slow cooker. Stir well. Cook on low for 4 hours. Simple & #Delish!

Cabbage Bake

¼ teaspoon dried basil leaves, crushed
¼ teaspoon ground black pepper
¼ teaspoon seasoned salt
½ cup water
½ teaspoon salt
¾ pound lean ground beef
1 (26 ounce) can chunky low-fat spaghetti sauce
1 cup long-grain rice
1 medium onion, finely chopped
6 cups shredded cabbage and carrots

Lightly brown ground beef in a skillet and drain fat. Set aside and cool. Place ½ of the cabbage and carrots in a slow cooker. Crumble ground beef over the top. Sprinkle ¼ teaspoon of the salt and 1/8 teaspoon of the pepper. Evenly incorporate onion, then rice over all. Top with remaining cabbage, salt, and pepper. Combine spaghetti sauce, water, basil, and seasoned salt; pour over cabbage. Cover and cook on low 5 to 6 hours or until rice is tender. Serve hot and enjoy!

Candied Bananas

¼ cup butter or margarine, melted
¼ cup lemon juice
¼ teaspoon salt
½ cup dark corn syrup
½ cup flaked coconut
½ teaspoons cinnamon
2 teaspoons grated lemon peel
6 green-tipped bananas, peeled

Put bananas and coconut into large enough slow cooker to fit in single layer. Sprinkle with cinnamon and salt. Mix corn syrup, butter, lemon peel, and lemon juice; pour over bananas. Cover and cook on low for 1 to 2 hours. #Delish!

Carrot Pudding

¼ teaspoon nutmeg
½ teaspoon salt
1 cup milk
1 small onion, grated
1 tablespoon sugar
3 eggs, beaten
4 large carrots, cooked and grated

Mix together carrots, onion, salt, nutmeg, sugar, milk, and eggs. Pour into slow cooker on highest setting for 3-4 hours. Simple & #Delish!

Cherry Cobbler

½ cup chopped nuts of your choice
½ teaspoon cinnamon
1 egg
1 package cake mix for 1 layer cake, or sweet muffin mix
1 (16 ounce) can light cherry pie filling
3 tablespoons evaporated milk

Place pie filling into a lightly buttered slow cooker and cook on high for 30 minutes. Mix together the remaining ingredients and spoon onto the hot pie filling. Cover and cook for 2 to 3 hours on low until fragrant and done. #Delish!

Chicken Casserole
½ cup chicken broth
½ cup diced celery
½ cup diced green pepper
½ cup diced onion
½ cup parmesan cheese
½ teaspoon basil
1½ cups cream-style cottage cheese
1 (4 ounce) can mushrooms
1 (4 ounce) jar pimiento
1 (8 ounce) package egg noodles
1 can cream of chicken soup
1 cup grated sharp process cheese
2 tablespoons melted butter
3 cups diced cooked chicken

Cook noodles according to package directions and drain and rinse thoroughly. In a large bowl, combine remaining ingredients with noodles until well mixed. Pour mixture into greased slow cooker. Cover and cook on low for 6-8 hours or on high for 3-4 hours. Enjoy!

Chicken Sensation
½ cup chicken broth or white wine
½ teaspoons black pepper
1 teaspoon basil
2 carrots, sliced
2 celery stalks with leaves,
2 onions, sliced
2 teaspoons salt
3 lbs. whole chicken, thawed

Put carrots, onions, and celery in bottom of slow cooker. Add whole chicken. Top with salt, pepper, liquid. Sprinkle basil over top. Cover and cook on low until done, about 8 to 10 hours. Enjoy!

Chocolate Brownie Pudding Cake
¼ cup peanut butter
¼ cup water
¼ to ½ cup milk chocolate chips
½ cup brown sugar
¾ cup water
1 large egg
1 tablespoon soft margarine
2½ cups brownie mix

2 tablespoons cocoa

Combine ¾ cup water, brown sugar, and cocoa in a saucepan. Bring to a boil. In the meantime combine the remaining ingredients in a small bowl. Whisk together or mix well with a spoon. Spread the batter evenly in the bottom of a lightly buttered slow cooker. Pour boiling mixture over the batter and cover. Cook on high about 2 hours; turn heat off and let stand for 30 minutes Spoon into dessert dishes while warm; serve with whipped cream or ice cream. #Delish!

Chops in a Crock

1 (10.5 ounce) can cream of mushroom soup
1 onion, chopped
2 teaspoons Worcestershire sauce
3 tablespoons catsup
6 pork chops (pre-browned for best flavor)

Place all ingredients into slow cooker and simmer for 4-5 hours. Serve with rice, noodles or mashed potatoes. Simple & #Delish!

Cola Basted Ham

¼ cup Pepsi or Coca-Cola
½ cup brown sugar
1 teaspoon dry mustard
3 - 4 pound pre-cooked ham

Combine brown sugar and mustard; moisten with just enough cola to create a smooth paste. Score the ham with shallow slashes in a diamond pattern. Rub ham with sugar mixture and place in slow cooker; add remaining cola. Cover and cook on high for 1 hour, then turn to low and cook for 6 to 7 hours. #Delish!

Cold Season Chicken Soup

¼ teaspoon leaf thyme
¼ teaspoon pepper
½ teaspoon basil
1 2½ - 3 lbs. whole fryer
1 cup noodles
1 package (10 ounces) frozen peas
2 onions, chopped
2 stalks celery, sliced
2 teaspoons salt
3 carrots, sliced
3 tablespoons dry parsley flakes
4 cups water or chicken stock

Place all ingredients in slow cooker, except noodles. Cover and cook on low for 8 to 10 hours or on high for 4 to 6 hours. One hour before serving, remove chicken and cool slightly. Remove meat from bones and return meat to slow cooker. Add noodles, cover and cook on high for 1 hour. Enjoy!

Country Citrus Fish
1½ lb. fish fillets of choice
1 medium onion, chopped
2 teaspoons grated lemon rind
2 teaspoons grated orange rind
4 teaspoons oil
5 tablespoons chopped parsley
Orange and lemon slices
Lawry's Season Salt (or plain salt/pepper) to taste

Butter a slow cooker and season fish to taste. Then place fish in pot. Put onion, parsley and grated rinds and oil over fish. Cover and cook on low for 1½ hours. Serve garnished with orange and lemon slices. Enjoy!

Cranberry Holiday Pork Roast
¼ teaspoon crushed red pepper
½ cup coarsely chopped dried apricots
½ cup sugar
1 can (16 ounce) whole-berry cranberry sauce
1 can (5.5 ounce) apricot nectar
1 medium onion, coarsely chopped
1 teaspoon dry mustard
4 medium potatoes, peeled and cut into 1" chunks

One 3-pound boneless center-cut pork loin roast, rolled and tied. Place the potatoes in slow cooker, then place the roast over the potatoes. In a large bowl, combine the remaining ingredients; mix well and pour over the roast. Cover and cook on the low setting for 5 to 6 hours. Remove roast, place on a cutting board and thinly slice. Serve with potatoes and watch it disappear. #Delish!

Crazy Cajun Pecans
¼ teaspoon cayenne pepper
¼ teaspoon garlic powder
½ teaspoon onion powder
1 pound pecan halves
1 tablespoon chili powder
1 teaspoon dried basil
1 teaspoon dried oregano
1 teaspoon dried thyme

1 teaspoon salt
4 tablespoons butter, melted
Combine all ingredients in slow cooker. Cover and cook on high for 15 minutes. Cook on low, uncovered, stirring occasionally for 2 hours. Transfer nuts to a baking sheet and cool completely. #Delish!

Cream of Sweet Potato Soup
1 teaspoon sugar
1/8 teaspoon each - ground cloves and nutmeg
1½ cup half-and-half or milk
2 cup chicken bouillon
3 sweet potatoes, peeled and sliced
Salt to taste
Put sweet potatoes and bouillon into slow cooker. Cover and cook on high 2 to 3 hours or until potatoes are tender. Puree in blender. Put back in cooker with remaining ingredients. Cover and cook on high 1 to 2 hours. Serve hot or chilled with a dollop of sour cream (optional). Enjoy!

Creamed Chicken & Rice
1 tablespoon olive oil
1 tablespoon whole thyme, crushed
Boneless chicken tenders (3 per person)
Broccoli florets
Cream of mushroom soup (1 can for 2-3 people, 2 for 4-6)
Diced red pepper
Long grain brown rice (1 cup per can of soup)
Onion soup mix (1 per each can of soup)
Salt and pepper to taste
Empty can of soup into a measuring cup and add water to equal 2½ cups (the extra is for the onion soup mix). Heat olive oil in a sauté pan and add rice until it begins to crackle. *Do not allow it to brown.* Whisk together the soups and extra water and seasonings as desired. Combine all ingredients (except veggies) in a slow cooker set to high and cook for 4-6 hours, or 8-10 hours on low. During last 30-45 minutes, add desired veggies. Pair with a bright tossed salad for a great meal. Enjoy!

Creamy Red Potatoes
1 tablespoon milk
1 can cream of potato soup, undiluted
1 envelope ranch salad dressing mix
2 lbs. small red potatoes, quartered
2 packages (8 ounces) cream cheese, softened
In a small bowl, beat cream cheese, soup, and salad dressing mix. Place potatoes in a slow cooker and pour mixture on top. Add a tablespoon of milk. Cover and cook on low for 8 hours or until potatoes are tender. #Delish!

Crockpot Black-Eyed Peas
1 bag (16 ounces) of dried black-eyed peas
1 small ham hock
1 (14.5 ounce) can of diced tomatoes with jalapenos
1 (14.5 ounce) can of diced tomatoes with mild green chilies
2 (10.5 ounce) cans of chicken broth
1 stalk of celery, chopped
Salt and pepper to taste
Pre-soak black-eyed peas for a few hours. Combine all ingredients and cook on low for 8-10 hours. #Delish!

Crockpot Chicken & Dumplings
½ cup heavy cream
½ teaspoon ground allspice
1 can refrigerated biscuits
1 cup dry white wine (optional)
1 onion, chopped
1 tablespoon minced parsley
1 tablespoon vegetable oil
1 teaspoon black pepper
2 medium carrots, peeled, sliced
2 cups chicken broth
2 stalks celery
2 tablespoons flour
3 pounds your favorite chicken parts -- cut up
4 tablespoons butter
Salt to taste
In a large skillet, brown onion in butter and oil just until tender; brown chicken parts and place all in a large slow cooker. Add remaining ingredients, except heavy cream, flour and biscuits. Cook on high for about 3 hours or on low for 5 to 7 hours. When chicken is done, plate pieces and allow them cool. Debone the chicken. Mix flour and cream together and add to slow cooker.

Open biscuits and cut each into 4 pieces. Drop into slow cooker and turn on high. Cook for about 30 minutes, until firm. Return deboned chicken meat to pot, allowing all flavors to comingle. Serve hot and enjoy!

Crockpot Clam Bisque

1 onion, chopped & sautéed
1 quart half and half
1 stick butter
2 cans minced clams with juice
4 cans of cream of potato soup

Sauté onions in butter, then add all ingredients in slow cooker for 4 hours on high or all day on low. #Delish!

Crockpot Jambalaya

½ cup white wine
1 cup chicken broth
1 green pepper, chopped
1 medium onion, chopped
1 pound chicken breasts, boneless and cut in 1" cubes
1 pound shrimp, cooked
1 pound smoked sausage, sliced
1 teaspoon cayenne pepper
2 cups rice, cooked
2 teaspoons Cajun seasoning
2 teaspoons oregano
2 teaspoons parsley
28 ounces crushed tomatoes

Cut chicken and slice sausage. Chop onion and green pepper. Put these into slow cooker and add remaining ingredients, except shrimp and rice. Cook on low for 6-8 hours or on high for 3-4 hours. 30 minutes before eating, add cooked shrimp and cooked rice; allow time for flavors to meld and dish to fully heat before serving with fresh cornbread. #Delish!

Curried Fruit Bake

½ teaspoon curry powder
1 can sliced peaches
1 cup packed brown sugar
1 package (11 ounces) dried apricots
1 package (16 ounces) prunes, pitted
14 ounces of ginger ale
2 cans (13 ½ ounces) pineapple chunks

Combine all ingredients in slow cooker. Cover and cook on low 4-5 hours or auto 3 hours. Enjoy!

Down Home Sausage & Rice

¼ to ½ teaspoon hot pepper sauce
½ cup chopped parsley (optional)
1 (14 ½ ounce) can diced tomatoes with liquid
1 cup uncooked instant rice
1 medium green pepper, diced
1 medium onion, diced
1 tablespoon chicken bouillon granules
1 tablespoon steak sauce
1 teaspoon sugar
2 celery stalks, thinly sliced
3 bay leaves or 1 teaspoon dried thyme
8 ounce kielbasa sausage, cut in ¼" slices

Combine sausage, tomatoes, onion, green pepper, celery bouillon, steak sauce, bay leaves, sugar and hot pepper sauce in slow cooker. Cover and cook on lowest setting for 8 hours. Remove bay leaves; stir in rice and ½ cup of water. Cook an additional 25 minutes. Stir in parsley if desired. #Delish!

Family Reunion Potato Salad

¼ cup green peppers, diced
¼ cup oil
¼ cup vinegar
½ cup celery sliced
½ cup onions, chopped
2 potatoes, sliced
Chopped parsley
Sliced bacon, cooked and crumbled

Combine all ingredients, except parsley and bacon, in a slow cooker. Add salt and pepper to taste. Stir and cook for 5-6 hours. *Add sugar to taste if needed.* Garnish with bacon and parsley. #Delish!

Garlic Chicken & Cabbage

½ red or white onion, chopped
1 whole chicken
Garlic salt/powder to your liking
Salt and pepper to taste

Season chicken and place in slow cooker. Add onion, garlic, pepper and salt. Fill slow cooker ¼-way with water, cover and cook on high 6-8 hours or until chicken begins to fall off the bone. During the final hour of cooking the chicken, cut up 1 head of green or red cabbage removing core, and place in a large pot of pan with no more than ½ to 1 cup water. Add two tablespoons of butter or margarine and sprinkle liberally with garlic salt and pepper. Cover and cook on med-high heat for 20-30 minutes. Once both chicken and cabbage are done, place cabbage in a bowl and top with chicken. Serve hot with cornbread. #Delish!

Ham & Cheese Casserole

1 can condensed cream of mushroom soup, undiluted
1 celery rib, chopped
1 cup milk
1 cup uncooked instant rice
1 jar (8 ounces) process cheese sauce
1 package (16 ounces) frozen broccoli cuts, thawed and drained
1 small onion, chopped
3 cups cubed fully cooked ham

In a slow cooker, combine broccoli and ham. Combine the soup, cheese sauce, milk, instant rice, celery and onion; stir into the broccoli mixture. Cover and cook on low 4-5 hours or until rice is tender. Enjoy!

Hamburger Casserole

1 can cream of chicken soup
1 can peas, drained
1 can water
2 lbs. browned ground beef
2 onions, sliced
2 stalks celery, diced
3 carrots, peeled and sliced
4 potatoes, peeled and sliced

Place potatoes in bottom of slow cooker and top with carrots and other vegetables. Place ground beef on top. Combine soup and water and pour over ground beef. Cover and cook on low for 6 to 8 hours. #Delish!

Home-Style Bread Pudding
¼ teaspoon salt
½ cup brown sugar
½ cup raisins or chopped dates
½ teaspoon cinnamon
1 teaspoon vanilla
2 ¼ cups milk
2 cups 1-inch bread cubes
2 eggs, slightly beaten

In medium mixing bowl, combine eggs with milk, vanilla, cinnamon, salt, bread, sugar, and raisins or dates. Pour into a baking or soufflé dish. Place a ring of aluminum foil in the bottom of the slow cooker to rest the dish on and add ½ cup hot water. Set baking dish on your aluminum foil trivet. Cover pot; cook on high for about 2 hours. Serve pudding warm or cool. Enjoy!

Hoppin' Shrimp Creole
¼ teaspoons pepper
¾ cup chopped bell pepper
1 (28 ounce) can whole tomatoes
1 (8 ounce) can tomato sauce
1 ¼ cup chopped onion
1½ cup diced celery
1 clove garlic or ¼ teaspoon garlic powder
1 lb. shrimp, deveined and shelled
1 teaspoon salt
6 drops Tabasco sauce

Combine all ingredients in slow cooker, except shrimp. Cook 3 - 4 hours on high or 6 - 8 hours on low. Add shrimp during the last hour of cooking. Serve over hot rice. *Chicken, rabbit or crawfish may be substituted for the shrimp.* Enjoy!

Hot 'N' Spicy Peanuts
¼ cup butter, cut in pieces
½ teaspoon garlic powder
½ teaspoon onion salt
2 teaspoons chili powder
6 cups raw peanuts, shelled

Place butter into slow cooker and heat, uncovered, on high until melted (15 to 20 minutes). Add nuts; stir to coat. Cover and cook on high for 30 minutes. Uncover and cook on high for 2½ hours longer, stirring occasionally. Sprinkle seasonings over nuts and toss to coat. Spread on a baking sheet to cool. These beauties will store in an airtight container in the refrigerator for up to 6 weeks. Serve at room temp or warmed. #Delish!

Jammin' Jerk Chicken
½ teaspoon ground allspice
½ to 1 habanero pepper, seeded, deveined, and finely minced *(wear gloves)*
1 heaping tablespoon chopped, crystallized ginger
1 large onion, cut into 8 pieces
1 teaspoon freshly ground black pepper
2 cloves garlic, crushed and minced
2 tablespoons dry mustard
2 tablespoons red wine or balsamic vinegar
2 tablespoons soy sauce
3 to 4 pounds chicken tenders

Combine onion and ginger in a food processor or blender and blend until finely chopped. Add remaining ingredients, except chicken, and pulse until well combined. Place chicken in slow cooker and cover with sauce. Cover and cook on low for 6 to 8 hours or on high for 3 to 4 hours. Meat will break apart effortlessly when done. #Delish!

Lemon Baked Chicken
16 ounces skinned and boned uncooked chicken breasts, cut into 4 pieces
1 lemon
1 teaspoon lemon pepper
1 teaspoon paprika

Place chicken pieces in a slow cooker. Squeeze juice of half a lemon over chicken. Sprinkle lemon pepper and paprika over top. Cut remaining lemon half into thin slices. Arrange slices around chicken. Cover and cook on high for 4 hours. Enjoy!

Lemon-Garlic Chicken
½ cup garlic cloves, crushed
½ cup lemon juice
1 cup white wine
1 teaspoon poultry seasoning
1 teaspoon seasoned salt
2 dashes tabasco
3 pounds chicken

Skin and cut up chicken. Combine with other ingredients in slow cooker/Crock Pot. Set on low for 4-5 hours. Debone chicken and serve over hot rice. #Delish!

Maple Sweet Potatoes

¼ cup apple cider
¼ cup brown sugar
¼ cup pure maple syrup
5 medium sweet potatoes
Dash salt and pepper to taste

Peel sweet potatoes and cut into ¼ to ½-inch thick slices; place in slow cooker. Whisk remaining ingredients together and pour over potatoes. Cover and cook on low 7 to 9 hours. Stir a few times, if possible, to keep them coated. Enjoy!

Melty Mac & Cheese

½ teaspoon black pepper
1½ cups milk
1 can (12 ounces) evaporated milk
1 teaspoon salt
2 eggs
4 cups (16 ounces) shredded sharp Cheddar Cheese
8 ounces elbow macaroni, cooked and drained

Place the cooked macaroni in a slow cooked sprayed with nonstick cooking spray. Add the remaining ingredients, except 1 cup of the cheese, and mix well. Sprinkle with the remaining 1 cup of cheese and then cover and cook on low for 5 to 6 hours or until the mixture is firm and golden around the edges. Enjoy!

Old-Fashioned Chicken Noodle Soup (Low-fat)

1 large onion, quartered
2 cans chicken broth
2 to 3 soup cans of water
3 boneless skinless chicken breast halves
3 carrots, peeled and cut into chunks
3 stalks celery, cut into chunks
8 ounces egg noodles
Dash of dried dill
Dash of dried parsley

Put vegetables in slow cooker. Add chicken. Pour in broth and water. Add dill and parsley. Cover and cook on low 8 hours. Remove veggies and chicken from slow cooker. Add egg noodles, turn to high and heat while you shred the chicken and mince the veggies. Return chicken and veggies to cups and heat through. The soup is ready when noodles are tender. #Delish!

Orange Glazed Chicken (Low-Fat)

¼ cup cold water
½ teaspoon marjoram
1 dash garlic powder (optional)
1 dash ground nutmeg
2 tablespoons cornstarch
3 chicken breasts, split
6 ounces orange juice, frozen concentrate-thawed

Combine thawed orange juice concentrate (not regular orange juice) in a bowl along with the marjoram, garlic powder and nutmeg. Split the chicken breasts to make 6 serving sizes. Dip pieces into the orange juice to coat completely. Place in slow cooker and pour the remaining OJ mixture over the chicken. Cover and cook on low for 7-9 hours, or cook on high for 4 hours. When done, remove chicken and place on a serving platter. Pour the sauce that remains into a saucepan. Mix the cornstarch and water and stir into the juice in pan. Cook over medium heat, stirring constantly, until thick and bubbly. Serve the sauce over the chicken with rice or potatoes. Enjoy!

Peach Crisp

½ cup flour
½ cup quick-cooking oats
1 can (21 ounces) peach pie filling
1 teaspoon brown sugar
1/3 cup butter, softened
2/3 cup brown sugar

Lightly butter a slow cooker. Place cherry pie filling in the slow cooker. Next, combine dry ingredients and mix well; cut in butter with a fork. Sprinkle crumbs over the pie filling. Cook for 5 hours on low. #Delish!

Salmon Bake

½ cup whole milk
1 can cream of celery soup
1 can cream of onion soup
1 can tomatoes, pureed in blender
1 green pepper, chopped
2 chicken bouillon cubes, crushed
3 cans pink salmon, deboned
3 teaspoons lemon juice
4 cups (about 10 slices) soft bread crumbs
6 eggs, well beaten

Grease walls of slow cooker with vegetable oil or nonstick cooking spray. Combine all ingredients, except celery soup and milk. Cover and cook on low 4-

6 hours or high for 3 hours. Next, combine cream of celery soup with ½ cup of milk and heat in saucepan. Use as sauce for salmon bake. Enjoy!

Saturday Night Dump Dinner
1/8 teaspoon pepper
¼ cup butter
¼ cup flour
½ cup flour
1 clove garlic, minced
1 onion, sliced
1 teaspoon salt
2 cups beer
2-3 lbs. boneless chuck, cut into 1 inch cubes

Coat beef cubes in ½ cup flour. Brown in melted butter; drain off excess fat. Next, combine browned meat with onion, salt, pepper, garlic, and beer in slow cooker. Cover and cook on low for 5-7 hours until meat is tender. Set slow cooker to high and dissolve remaining ¼ cup flour in small amount of water. Stir into the meat mixture and cook on high 30-40 minutes. Serve with rice and a fresh green salad. #Delish!

Savory Corn Cake
½ cup sour cream
1 can (4 ounces) chopped green chilies, undrained
1 can (15 ounces) creamed corn
2 boxes (8 ounces) corn muffin mix
2 large eggs
2 tablespoons soft margarine
3 to 4 tablespoons chunky salsa

In a medium bowl, combine creamed corn, eggs, sour cream, chilies, and margarine. Whisk together until well combined. Add corn muffin mix, stirring well to combine. Generously grease the walls of slow cooker with margarine or butter. Pour batter into the slow cooker and spoon salsa over the top and cut into the batter. Cover and cook on high for about 2½ hours. Turn heat off and let cool with lid ajar, for about 15 minutes. Loosen sides with a knife and invert onto a large plate. If a little of the top sticks to the bottom of the pot, dollop a little salsa on the top. Garnish with sour cream and chopped green onion. #Delish!

Seafood Chowder

¼ lb. bacon or salt pork, diced
¼ teaspoons pepper
1½ teaspoons salt
1 can evaporated milk
1 medium onion, chopped
2 cups water
2 lbs. frozen fish filets
4 medium potatoes, peeled and cubed

Thaw frozen fish in refrigerator. Cut into bite-sized pieces. In skillet, sauté bacon or salt pork and onion until meat is cooked and onion is golden. Drain and put into slow cooker with the fish pieces. Add potatoes, water, salt and pepper. Cover and cook on low for 6 - 9 hours. Add evaporated milk during last hour. If the chowder is thicker than you like, add more milk (any type will do). Serve hot. Enjoy!

Simple Sunday Roast

1 cup water
2½ lbs. chuck roast
2 packets dry Italian dressing mix or ranch dressing mix

Place beef in slow cooker, sprinkle seasonings over meat, pour water over all. Cook on low 6-8 hours or until meat shreds easily. Simple and #Delish!

Slow-Cooker Candy

12 ounce package of semi-sweet chocolate chips
2 lbs. white almond bark
24 ounce jar dry roasted peanuts
4 ounce bar of chocolate

Put all ingredients in slow cooker; cook 1 hour on high. Do not stir. Set to low and stir every 15 minutes for 1 hour. Pour mixture onto waxed paper and cool. Break into nice size pieces and store in an air-tight container. #Delish!

Southern Barbecue Chicken

½ cup brown sugar
½ cup white vinegar
½ teaspoon garlic powder
½ teaspoon red pepper flakes
1 bottle favorite BBQ sauce
1 teaspoon mesquite seasoning
4-6 boneless chicken breasts

Mix BBQ sauce with all seasonings. Place rinsed chicken pieces in slow cooker. Pour sauce over all. Cook on low for 4 ½ hours in crock pot about 4-6 hours. Serve with baked beans, potato salad and coleslaw. #Delish!

Southern Style Green Bean & Potato Casserole

1 can cream of celery soup
2 tablespoons minced dried onion
4 to 5 cups whole fresh green beans, trimmed
4 to 6 medium red potatoes, sliced about ¼" thick (peeled or unpeeled)
6 slices bacon, diced fried and drained
Salt and pepper to taste

Place sliced potatoes and green beans in slow cooker; add other ingredients. Cover and cook on low 7 to 9 hours. #Delish!

Spicy BBQ Beef Stew

¼ cup cold water
½ cup green pepper, chopped
½ teaspoon salt
1 can (4 ounces) mushrooms
1 can (8 ounces) tomatoes
1 cup onion, sliced
1 large clove garlic
1/3 cup barbecue sauce
1/8 teaspoon pepper
2 cups beef stock
2 lbs. stew meat
3 tablespoons cornstarch
3 tablespoons oil

Sauté onion, pepper and garlic in oil. Add salt, pepper, beef stock, tomatoes, mushrooms, and barbecue sauce. Cook in slow cooker on low heat 8-10 hours. Mix cornstarch with cold water and thicken before serving. Serve over savory cooked rice. #Delish!

Split Pea Soup

¼ cups fresh parsley, chopped
½ teaspoons fresh pepper
1 (16 ounce) package dried green split peas, rinsed
1 bay leaf
1 hambone, or 2 meaty hammocks, or 2 cups diced ham
1 medium onion, chopped
1 or 2 cloves of garlic, minced
1 tablespoon seasoned salt
1½ quarts hot water
2 stalks of celery plus leaves, chopped
3 carrots, peeled & sliced

Layer ingredients in slow cooker, pour in water. Do not stir. Cover and cook on high 4 to 5 hours or on low 8 to 10 hours until peas are very soft and ham falls easily from the bone. Remove bones and bay leaf. Serve garnished with croutons. #Delish!

Spoon Peaches

1/3 cup sugar
½ can evaporated milk
½ cup brown sugar
¾ cup Bisquik mix
¾ teaspoons cinnamon
2 cups peaches, mashed
2 eggs
2 teaspoons margarine, melted
2 teaspoons vanilla

Spray slow cooker with non-stick cooking spray. Combine sugars and Bisquik. Add eggs, vanilla, melted margarine and milk. Add peaches and cinnamon. Pour all into a slow cooker and set to low for 6 to 8 hours. Enjoy!

Tasty Tenderloin Tips

1 lb. tenderloin tips
1 can mushroom soup
1 package onion soup mix
¼ cups water

Combine ingredients in a slow cooker. Cook on low for 8 hours. Serve over buttered/seasoned egg noodles and enjoy!

Vegetable Beef Soup

1 (16 ounces) can cut green beans
1 cup chopped celery
1 cup chopped onion
1 cup sliced carrots
1 large (28 ounces) can whole tomatoes, chopped
1 pound ground chuck
1 teaspoon salt
1 teaspoon Worcestershire sauce
2 (10 ½ ounces) cans condensed beef bouillon
2 teaspoon chili powder
2-3 dashes cayenne pepper sauce
3 cup diced potatoes

Brown meat with onion and celery; drain fat. Stir in remaining ingredients and add 1 or 2 cups water. Cover and cook on low for 8-10 hours.

Thank you for your purchase!
May you enjoy and be well!

ABOUT THE AUTHOR

I am a Tennessee native and a connoisseur of great tastes. My culinary delights are inspired by my Southern roots.

I am from cornbread and cabbage, fried chicken and Kool-Aid soaked lemon slices.

I am from hen houses, persimmon trees and juicy, red tomatoes on the vine.

I am from sunflowers growing wild in summer and homemade ice cream in the winter.

I am from family reunions, blue collar men, happy housewives, and Sunday dinners.

I am from spiritual folks who didn't always get it right, but believed in the power of prayer – and taught it to their kids.

I am from the hottest of hot summers and kids running barefoot and free through thirsty Tennessee grass.

I am from a grandmother who sang gospel that was magic...song drenched air would tumble from her lungs, leap into your spirit and make you feel fantastic things.

I am from hard, heartfelt lessons about living and kitchens full of the perfume of love.

♥♥♥ *This book is from my heart to yours.* ♥♥♥

Find more cookbooks online at http://www.tinyurl.com/sodelishdish.
For freebies & new book announcements, follow @SoDelishDish on social media!

Scan with your smartphone!

Printed in Great Britain
by Amazon